The Villages of England by A.K. Wickham was first published by B.T. Batsford in 1932. The dust jacket illustration of the village of Kersey in Suffolk by Brian Cook was part of the innovative *English Life* series published by Batsford through the 1930s, 40s and 50s.

Brian Cook's illustrations of Britain and its cottages, churches, villages and landscapes during these decades are now iconic and highlight the best of Britain. His heightened use of colour and flat poster style has been much imitated but never surpassed. A comprehensive collection of his dust jacket illustrations are published in *Brian Cook's Landscapes of Britain* (Batsford, 2010).

Eurythmic

California

First published in the
United Kingdom in 2011 by
Anova Books Ltd
10 Southcombe Street
London W14 0RA

Copyright © Anova Books, 2011

www.anovabooks.com

10 9 8 7 6 5 4 3 2 1

Printed in China